THEN & NOW

CONSHOHOCKEN

This rare photograph of the Washington Fire Company was taken in 1924 through a side yard located on West Hector Street. The Washington Fire Company was founded in 1873 and chartered in 1874 with 40 members. At the time of this photograph, trolley cars were running up and down Fayette Street, and Conshohocken had 15 registered hotels in the borough. The firehouse was active for more than 110 years before the members moved into their new quarters, located behind the original firehouse on West Elm Street. (Photograph from the collection of Jack Coll.)

THEN & NOW

CONSHOHOCKEN

Jack and Brian Coll

ARCADIA
PUBLISHING

Published by Arcadia Publishing
Charleston, South Carolina

Printed in the United States of America

Library of Congress Catalog Card Number: 2004107287

Then and Now is a registered trademark and is used under license from
Salamander Books Limited

For all general information contact Arcadia Publishing at:
Telephone 843-853-2070
Fax 843-853-0044
E-mail sales@arcadiapublishing.com
For customer service and orders:
Toll-Free 1-888-313-2665

Visit us on the Internet at www.arcadiapublishing.com

On the cover: In 1956, St. Matthew Grade School was located on East Hector Street in a building constructed in 1861. The school is now located in the 200 block of Fayette Street. In 1996, St. Matthew's merged with SS. Cosmas, Damian School, and St. Mary's and was renamed Conshohocken Catholic. Sr. Sharon McCarthy stands proudly with members of her fifth-grade class. She noted that while the photographs are nearly 50 years separated, the school has always been built on a firm educational foundation. (Photograph by Brian Coll, 2004.)

Children play on the merry-go-round at Mary Jane Sutcliffe Park, located on the west side of the borough. The 37-acre park, dedicated on July 4, 1930, was donated by the late Frank Sutcliffe in honor of his wife, Mary Jane. The photograph was taken in the mid-1940s. (Photograph from the collection of Jack Coll.)

CONTENTS

ACKNOWLEDGMENTS

Over the past 30 years, residents of this wonderful community have opened their hearts and scrapbooks to us, lending and passing along snapshots of Conshohocken. Although many of these residents have since left us, their photographs live on in *Conshohocken*.

We would like to thank Dr. Eugene Katz, John "Chick" McCarter, Harold McCuen, Alan Worth, Tom Carroll, George Rafferty, Sam and Herb Webster, Gene Walsh, Paul Price, George Rissell, the Conshohocken Historical Society, and the Marriott Hotel West Conshohocken. Special thanks go to Dr. Joseph Leary, who for years inspired and guided me with his extensive knowledge of Conshohocken.

Thanks to Donna for all her help along the way, and thanks to Conshohocken mayor Bob Frost for his kind introduction.

This book is dedicated to the citizens of Conshohocken who have shared the history of this great borough, including the late Chris Bockrath, Art Andrey, Tony Santoni, Joe Lewis, Ange D'Amico, John Borusiewicz, Chick McCarter, Bill Collins, and Dr. Joseph Leary.

INTRODUCTION

Conshohocken, incorporated more than 150 years ago, has gone through some incredible changes throughout its relatively short life span. Prior to its incorporation, the approximate one square mile of land was inhabited by the Native Americans of the Lenni Lenape nation. After William Penn purchased the land, it did not take long for the founding fathers to realize that, along with its prime location along the Schuylkill River and its proximity to the Philadelphia markets, there were some huge opportunities to consider. Thirty years later, Conshohocken was a bustling industrial community made of many manufacturing plants and mills, including Alan Wood Steel Company, Lee Tires, and Walker Brothers, all facilities that became known throughout the world. These plants and mills, employing thousands, allowed generations of families to live, grow, and prosper as Conshohocken evolved.

Prosperity takes ongoing planning, and by the early 1960s, the borough had started a downward business spiral. Almost all of the factories and mills were boarded up, closed, and abandoned. Without the larger businesses to support the workers, many of the local mom-and-pop businesses also fell by the wayside. The lower end of town, once a bustling hub of activity lined with stores and restaurants, now resembled a ghost town.

In the 1970s, an opportunity arose that the town's forefathers recognized as a way to reestablish Conshohocken as the thriving community it once was. A program established by the federal government allowed money to be loaned out to developers who would enter into an agreement to revive abandoned mills and properties. It seemed custom fit for Conshohocken. They say that history repeats itself, and those developers also realized that the location of the town, with its access to the Schuylkill River and proximity to Philadelphia, was again a key factor and a major selling point.

Twenty-five years of continued progress has brought Conshohocken into the 21st century with no end in sight, as development throughout the town and along the river is scheduled to continue for the foreseeable future. Conshohocken has now become the business center for Montgomery County and is a much coveted area for businesses and families to call home.

As expected, an immeasurable amount of change has occurred throughout Conshohocken's history. Jack and Brian Coll have taken it upon themselves to present a collection of photographs representing the borough as it was then and how it is now. It is an excellent collection, stretching back over 150 years, that will allow old-timers to reminisce but will also allow the next generation to realize what once was. From the A Field to the Washies Fire Company, the Colls have encapsulated the growth of Conshohocken, from a blue-collar mill town in the 1800s to a bustling, thriving community in the 21st century.

—Mayor Robert Frost

Students from the Harry Street School are on a field trip to the Acme Market (later Light Parker Furniture), then located at East First Avenue and Fayette Street. Bessie Nace was the teacher when this photograph was taken on May 22, 1940.

This rare photograph of the rear of the Charles Lukens homestead shows Charles with his children sitting on the back porch steps. Charles, the son of Lewis Lukens, built his home on the corner of East Fifth Avenue and Fayette Street. Although he passed away in 1902, his family owned the property until the mid-1930s, when the federal government purchased the property and built a post office. The post office, opened in November 1940, has served this borough for nearly 65 years at that location. Fayette Street was named after General Lafayette of George Washington's army.

Chapter 1
THE HOUSES OF FAYETTE STREET

Lewis Augustus Lukens was born in Conshohocken in 1807 on his parents' farm, located on West Third Avenue and Maple Street. Lukens built a two-and-a-half-story Victorian Gothic Revival home (above) in 1857 on the corner of East Third Avenue and Fayette Street. The former town burgess passed away in 1898 at 91 years of age. Nine years later, his family gave his house and property to the borough of Conshohocken to be used as a library. The borough has taken very good care of the property, thanks in part to the library's board of directors. The library, founded in 1907, remains as one of Conshohocken's most prestigious buildings. (Left, photograph by Brian Coll, 2004.)

The 1914 photograph below, taken at the intersection of Fayette Street and East Third Avenue, shows the home of John Bowker. The property, consisting of the house, the stable, and four lots, was sold the same year this photograph was taken to James Gibney, who later transferred the deed to Catholic archbishop Edmond Francis Prendergast. Construction began in 1915 for the new St. Matthew's Catholic Church. St. Matthew's dedicated its new $80,000 church on September 21, 1919. The Bowker house was moved to the corner of East Third Avenue and Harry Street and is used as a convent. A second property next door to the Bowker home on Fayette Street was also purchased from John Pugh and

is currently occupied by St. Matthew's rectory. (Above, photograph by Brian Coll, 2004.)

SITE OF ST. MATTHEW'S NEW CHURCH, Fayette St. and 3rd Ave., Conshohocken,
Pub. for McCoy's Drug Stores, Conshohocken,

When St. Matthew's Church bought John Bowker's property, located on East Third Avenue and Fayette Street, in 1915, Bowker's house (above) was moved to the corner of East Third Avenue and Harry Street and was used as St. Matthew's convent for many years until it was replaced with a modern-day structure that now occupies the lot. (Left, photograph by Brian Coll, 2004.)

Members of the Davis family stand outside their house, once located on the northeast corner of East Fifth Avenue and Fayette Street. The family in the photograph, taken in the mid-1930s, includes Glen (the small child), Sam, Ed, and Bill. The house was demolished in the late 1950s and replaced by a gas station. A garage belonging to St. Mark's Lutheran Church can be seen on the right of the photograph. (Right, photograph by Brian Coll, 2004.)

William Perot Jr. and Annie Wood, daughter of David L. Wood and Mary Cumming Wood, married at the age of 18. They lived in their home on West Fifth Avenue and Fayette Street until William's death at the age of 75 in 1928. The Perot estate was then sold to Horace C. Jones, president of the First National Bank of Conshohocken. The bank was then located at West Hector and Fayette Streets. Jones sold the property to the First National Bank of Philadelphia in 1954. The house was razed, and a new bank building was erected. Today, the bank continues to serve the borough as Wachovia Bank. (Above, photograph from the collection of Jack Coll, 1954; left, photograph by Brian Coll, 2004.)

The Miraglia house, located at 528 Fayette Street, was built in 1854 by Squire Jones for Joseph Whitton. Whitton owned a large woolen mill on Washington Street along the river. Dr. Paul Miraglia and his wife, Eleanor, purchased the property in 1938, and law and tax offices now occupy the building. (Right, photograph by Brian Coll, 2004.)

The Jawood Lukens home (above), formerly located on the northeast corner of Sixth Avenue and Fayette Street, was one of three homes owned by the Lukens family on Fayette Street. The other two belonged to Charles (at Fifth Avenue) and Lewis (at East Third Avenue). Jawood's house was later used for offices, where Dr. Joseph Leary began his dental career. The building was demolished in the 1950s. It was replaced by a gas station, and the site is now occupied by a 7-11 store. (Left, photograph by Brian Coll, 2004.)

A Sunoco station once occupied the former site of the Jawood Lukens home, located on the northeast corner of Sixth Avenue and Fayette Street, but it was demolished in 1980. The 7-11 store was built in 1982 and remains a staple in the Conshohocken community.

The Harrison house, seen in this early-1950s photograph, was located on the corner of East Seventh Avenue and Fayette Street. For many years, Mr. Harrison owned a company located in West Conshohocken that made rugs and carpets. The house was demolished shortly after this photograph was taken, and an Acme Market was established there. Nearly 50 years later, Acme Markets sold the building to CVS pharmacy. The Harrison house was typical of the mansions that once graced the entire length of Fayette Street. (Left, photograph by Brian Coll, 2004.)

The O'Brian property was located on the northeast corner of Eighth Avenue and Fayette Street and was one of the many large and prominent homes that once graced Conshohocken's main street. In 1921, members of the Conshohocken Fritz Lodge No. 420 of the Free and Accepted Masons bought the property and, in 1929, constructed a temple at the cost of $46,640. After nearly two years of construction, the lodge opened in March 1931. (Right, photograph by Brian Coll, 2004.)

This beautiful mansion, owned by Henry Tracey, was located on the southwest corner of Eighth Avenue and Fayette Street and was known as Indianola. The house was built in the early part of the 20th century along with Tracey's brother's house, located at Seventh Avenue and Fayette Street and seen on the right side of the above photograph. The two properties were sold in 1955, along with a third property located on East Seventh Avenue, for $100,000 by St. Matthew's Church. Gas stations were built on both corners of Fayette Street, including a Getty and Exxon station. (Left, photograph by Brian Coll, 2004.)

The building that has served as Conshohocken's borough hall since 1964 is located on the southwest corner of Eighth Avenue and Fayette Street and was built in 1893 by Alexander Martin and Son. The 23-room mansion with an oversized carriage house was built for John Elwood Lee (1860–1914) and his wife, Jennie, whose maiden name was Cleaver. Lee made millions of dollars in the surgical supplies business before opening his tire factory on East Hector Street. The tire factory opened in 1909, and Lee's name and his tires became known worldwide. (Right, photograph by Brian Coll, 2004.)

Members of the Washington Fire Company march in one of the hundreds of parades the company has participated in since its incorporation in 1874. Notice the house on the left, one of two Tracey mansions on Fayette Street. This is the only known photograph to show George and Margaret Tracey's house located at East Seventh Avenue and Fayette Street, currently the location of an Exxon station. The second Tracy mansion was located next door at Eighth Avenue and Fayette Street, the current location of a Getty station.

The Acme Market building was constructed in the 1950s, when the former Harrison mansion was demolished. The market was on the left at Seventh Avenue and Fayette Street, and the A&P supermarket was on the right. The Acme Market remained for nearly 50 years, while the A&P building became home to many businesses, including Baby Town, Penn Jersey Auto Parts, and, currently, Staley Electric.

Chapter 2

THE BUSINESSES OF FAYETTE STREET

The Tradesmen's National Bank (above), once located on the northeast corner of Hector and Fayette Streets, was founded in 1882 and grew into one of Montgomery County's strongest banks. In September 1943, the bank closed its doors and transferred its assets across Fayette Street to the First National Bank of Conshohocken. In later years, the building served as Smith's Music store, a travel agency, and a few other retail outlets, before it was demolished in the late 1970s as part of urban renewal. It now serves the community as a parking lot. (Above, photograph from the collection of Jack Coll; left, photograph by Brian Coll, 2004.)

After more than 30 years as owners of the Conshohocken 401 Diner, Bill Danitz Sr. and Bill Danitz Jr. sold the family diner. The two owners (below) stood behind the counter on the final days, recalling good times, including the time that actor Carroll O'Connor (Archie Bunker) and his wife visited the diner one afternoon. The newly refurbished 401 Diner recently reopened with new owners, after being remodeled for more than two years. Standing behind the counter of the new 1950s-style diner are, from left to right, Tom Wallace, Mike Trotter, Rosie McFarland, Cathy Wallace, Malick Thiaw, Monica Kochran, Nadine McKeown, and Nancy Wright. (Right, photograph by Brian Coll, 2004.)

Taken in 1961, the photograph above shows Charles Hairstylist, at 324 Fayette Street. The building was the former office of Dr. James Hargreaves and is now occupied by Coll's Custom Framing. To the left was an insurance firm, currently occupied by WIPPS. To the right, at 326 Fayette Street, is Dougherty's Drug Store, which is now occupied by Al's Deli. (Left, photograph by Brian Coll, 2004.)

Shirley's Self Serve Market opened in the early 1930s at 106 Fayette Street. The market was later purchased by Edward S. Weiner and his wife, Shirley. (The name was already on the building.) The Weiners renamed it Shirley's Meat Market and maintained the business into the late 1960s before selling the building. The Win Wah Inn Restaurant now occupies 106 Fayette Street, and a new Thai restaurant opened at 108 Fayette Street. (Right, photograph by Brian Coll, 2004.)

Back in the early part of the 20th century, E. F. Moore's business was simply known as the Conshohocken Garage. The business repaired wagons and automobiles and sold Ford auto parts. E. F. Moore began the business on East First Avenue. By 1924, a Chevrolet franchise was obtained, as was an Oldsmobile franchise about 10 years later. This 1930s photograph was taken on 12th Avenue shortly after E. F. Moore Chevrolet moved the operation to its present location. As Moore's business approaches 90 years of service to the Conshohocken community, one can only wonder about the hundreds of satisfied customers. (Left, photograph by Brian Coll, 2004.)

Anthony's, a barbershop owned and operated by Anthony Lincul, was located at 8 East Hector Street. Posing with Lincul are, from left to right, Sam Glass, James Meeney, James "Yippy" Fondots, and Nick Talone. Lincul passed away in 1961 after cutting hair for 40 years. Anthony's lives on through his son Rudy, who has been cutting hair for 37 years at a shop at 316 Fayette Street. (Below, photograph courtesy of Rudy Lincul; right, photograph by Brian Coll, 2004.)

The Webster homestead (above), at 804 Fayette Street, and the McClure homestead, at 806 Fayette Street, were very early homes on the upper end of the street, known in 1899 (when this photograph was taken) as the Conshohocken–Plymouth Turnpike. The Webster home had a dairy farm on the property for many years. In the early 1930s, an attempt was made to put a gas station where the barn was located. The town objected, and the property remained a dairy barn. Today, the barn at West Eighth Avenue and Forrest Street is an apartment complex. The Brides Boutique is located at 804 Fayette Street, and at 806 Fayette Street is Nationwide Insurance, Freas Agency. (Left, photograph by Brian Coll, 2004.)

In 1919, a small candy store and an adjacent building were demolished at the corner of West First Avenue and Fayette Street. One and a half years later, on November 11, 1921, the Riant Theatre opened its doors there. A contest was held to name the new state-of-the-art theater, and the name Riant was submitted by George Chell, who resided on West First Avenue. *Riant* is a French word that means "laughing, smiling, pleasant, and cheerful." The first movie shown at the theater was *The Sign on the Door,* staring Norma Tallmadge. The first talkie came in 1928. After more than 50 years, in 1976, the Riant Theatre was demolished, and although a modern-day office building sits on the corner, the cherished landmark will be remembered by many thousands of

residents who attended the films in the old movie house. (Above, photograph by Brian Coll, 2004.)

Bob Crawford's cigar store was located on the corner of East Second Avenue and Fayette Street. It served as a place for steelworkers to gather for friendly conversation and a place to catch up on the latest gossip. A number of residents posing in front of Crawford's store include Bill Lukens, Bob Crawford, Tom Pope, George Koch, Bill Murray, Henry Wildfire, Luke McCall, Chris Montgomery, Andy Ling, Archie Hyde, Cliff Ramey, and Jay Pearson. Crawford's building was torn down in 1924 to make way for the Knights of Columbus building that now occupies the corner. The Hemcher family purchased the property and opened the Great American Pub, where customers gather for friendly conversation and a place to catch up of the latest town gossip. Members of the pub staff include Liz Koo, Jessica Driscoll, Kelly Day, Camille Fryday, Judy Prudente, Geri Magee, Dave Brigg, and Jackie Palumbo. (Left, photograph by Brian Coll, 2004.)

On November 11, 1918, the signing of the armistice at Complegne, France, brought a close to World War I. On November 11, 1928, Conshohocken dedicated the newly constructed monument located at West Second Avenue and Fayette Street with hundreds in attendance. Conshohocken residents had a lot to celebrate at the dedication because the federal government announced that the small borough of Conshohocken sent more men and women off to participate in World War I than any other community in the country per capita. In recent years, a small group of veterans and residents formed a group called CONVET, who raised more than $100,000 to remodel the monument that serves as a reminder of all men and women who served and

sacrificed for our country. To the left of the monument is the Conshohocken Trust Company Bank and several grocery stores. (Below, photograph from the collection of Jack Coll; above, photograph by Brian Coll, 2004.)

Paul Miller's Mortuary was originally located on East Third Avenue before it was moved to West Third Avenue and Fayette Street back in the early 1930s. The business was later owned by William T. Ardell, followed by his son-in-law George Snear. In recent years, Snear's Funeral Home merged with the Donald Moore Funeral Home and is currently called the Moore-Snear Funeral Home. (Left, photograph by Brian Coll, 2004.)

The Windmill was located for more than 25 years at East 11th Avenue and Fayette Street. Through the years, the Windmill was an office for a used-car lot, an ice-cream and candy store, an insurance office, and the office of a local carpenter and builder. This site is currently occupied by Pennsylvania state representative Melissa Murphy Weber's office. (Right, photograph by Brian Coll, 2004.)

In the fall of 1872, a small group of investors led by prominent manufacturer Alan Wood Jr. applied for a charter to establish a bank to be located on the southwest corner of Hector and Fayette Streets. A private residence owned by George Washington Jacoby was sold to the bank for $12,000, and in early 1873, the First National Bank of Conshohocken was opened for business. (Photograph from the collection of Alan Worth, 1923.)

In 1923, the original building of the First National Bank of Conshohocken was demolished. In 1924, a handsome marble structure (below) replaced it. In 1948, the bank celebrated 75 years of service to the community, and in 1956, a new building was built on the corner of Fifth Avenue and Fayette Street, which became the First National Bank of Philadelphia, followed by Core States, First Union, and currently Wachovia Bank. (Below, photograph from the collection of Jack Coll, 1940; right, photograph by Brian Coll, 2004.)

Conshohocken's post office is currently located on the southeast corner of Fifth Avenue and Fayette Street. The property was formerly owned by Charles Lukens. Lukens's house was demolished in 1938, and the U.S. Department of the Treasury in Washington, D.C., accepted the proposal to purchase the property for $13,000 in 1939. The building was erected by the Haupt Construction Company of Philadelphia. Subcontractors included F. B. Davidson, excavating; Frank Gravinese, stone work; George Wood, brick work; and Robert McFarland, plumbing and heating. When the new and improved post office opened in November 1940, the staff included a postmaster, assistant postmaster, four clerks, six carriers, one rural carrier, and three part-time carriers. The carriage house, now converted into offices, still remains from the old Lukens house and can be seen on Harry Street. (Above, photograph from the collection of Jack Coll; left, photograph by Brian Coll, 2004.)

Dave Little built this opera house and retail outlet on the northwest corner of First Avenue and Fayette Street. The opera house had seating with a stage area on the second floor where St. Matthew's and Conshohocken High School held their graduations at the beginning of the 20th century. Also, SS. Cosmas and Damian Church was founded in this building, and the Barnum and Bailey circus featured Tom Thumb along with his wife, Minnie, in an 1883 stage production on the second floor. The building was demolished in the early 1920s, and Woolworth's was built. Today, the former Woolworth building is home to Light Parker Furniture. (Below, photograph by Brian Coll, 2004.)

Light Parker Furniture has been a cornerstone in Conshohocken for more than half a century. Frank Parker and Jack Light founded the store in 1943 and, later, moved into the former Acme Market building, located on the southeast corner of First Avenue and Fayette Street in the mid-1950s. Prior to the Acme Market, the building was occupied by Bell's food store, which served the community for many years. (Above, photograph from the collection of Jack Coll; left, photograph by Brian Coll, 2004.)

This photograph of Bell's includes Sue Pennington (far left) and Edwin Skilton (standing next to her). Stephen Vecchio, a nephew of Frank Parker, is the current owner of Light Parker Furniture, and he runs a very successful furniture business just across the street. The site of the former Bell's store, Acme Market, and Light Parker Furniture is now a parking garage.

Conshohocken, long known as "the Iron Borough" because of the many steel mills along the river, boasted 230 retail businesses at one time, including Billy McGowen's cigar store, located at 66 Fayette Street. When this photograph was taken in 1900, McGowen's was known as "the Home of the Five Cent Cigar." McGowen is on the far left of the above photograph, standing next to his father. In the photograph to the left is the site on Fayette Street where McGowen's once stood alongside many other well-known establishments of the day.

McClement's pharmacy and Ciavarelli's Funeral Home were once located in the 500 block of Fayette Street in the early 1960s. McClement's Pharmacy became Mascio's pharmacy before closing in 2001. Ciavarelli's Funeral Home moved across the street. Both buildings are now occupied by offices.

Chapter 3

OTHER BUSINESSES OF CONSHOHOCKEN

The Desimone building, located at 4 and 6 East First Avenue, was built in 1926, after Cornelius A. Desimone purchased the property from Morris Kessler. He built two stores with modern offices on the second floor. Harry Keyser moved his café from the Riant Theatre, located just across Fayette Street, into the No. 4 storefront; Desimone occupied two of the offices on the second floor; and George A. Shaw, borough tax collector, occupied the back upstairs office. The building, now owned by Frank Dennis, contains the John A. Storti Jr. accounting firm on the first floor of 4 East First Avenue, Dennis and Dennis Attorneys at Law occupy the second floor, and Best Cleaners occupy the storefront at 6 East First Avenue. (Above, photograph from the collection of Jack Coll, 1926; left, photograph by Brian Coll, 2004.)

Nick Talone's beer–distribution business (below) was located at 12 East Hector Street. Talone poses outside his store in this late-19th-century photograph. More than 100 years later, Alex and David pose with their father Alex Piermani outside their beer-distribution business, located on East Second Avenue. Piermani started the business in 1944 at Sixth Avenue and Maple Street (currently B&M Auto Supplies). They then moved up Maple Street for a couple of years before moving to their current location on Second Avenue in December 1948. (Right, photograph by Brian Coll, 2004.)

More than half a century ago, George and Nick John posed for a photograph in front of their garage showing off their modern-day tow truck and service vehicle. The John Brothers Conshohocken motor service was located on First Avenue and Forrest Street. Today Bill John, son of George, operates the business with his sons on East Second Avenue. The Johns have serviced cars in Conshohocken for nearly 90 years. (Above, photograph from the collection of Jack Coll; left, photograph by Brian Coll, 2004.)

Pat McCoy's general store was located on the southwest corner of West Fourth Avenue and Harry Street. This photograph, taken in 1895, shows a busy intersection with a horse and wagon sitting in front of McCoy's. Corner stores were popular in every town in the county, as most residents had little or no means of transportation to purchase goods. The building has served as an apartment house for decades. (Right, photograph by Brian Coll, 2004.)

The former Demarco Bar (above) was located at 120 Fayette Street. Sammy Demarco's bar was an excellent watering hole for the locals to gather

and spread the news, solve the world's problems, and talk about the Phillies and the A's. The above photograph shows Demarco and his wife standing behind the bar they owned for many years. Today, Ed Cassidy owns and operates the CasMar Bar, located at Eighth Avenue and Harry Street. The family members seen in the present-day photograph are, from left to right, as follows: (front row) Liz, Debbie Mason, and Colleen Schlips; (back row) Ed, Danny, and Sean. The Cassidy family has owned the bar for the past 25 years. Today, locals gather to spread the news, solve the world's problems, and talk about the Phillies and Flyers. (Left, photograph by Brian Coll, 2004.)

This photograph of the Schuylkill Navigation Company Canal shows the John Wood Manufacturing Company as it was viewed nearly 80 years ago from the Matsonford Bridge. The canal was built from 1816 to 1824 and was the main reason the Alan Wood Steel Company opened for business in 1832, creating Montgomery County's largest employer for nearly a century. Today's view of Washington Street from the Matsonford Bridge shows massive office buildings where mules once pulled canal boats loaded with goods bound for the city of Philadelphia, where they were dispersed throughout the world. (Right, photograph by Brian Coll, 2004.)

More than a century ago, members of the Moore family purchased property on the corner of East First and Spring Mill Avenues where they meet Harry Street. The Moores opened a boarding stable, where road-weary travelers could rest their horses and freshen up.

By 1915, horseless carriages were crowding the dirt roads throughout the country. Henry Ford was building automobiles by the thousands, and the Moore family went into the automobile parts and service business selling Ford parts. Some years later, the automobile operation moved uptown to 12th Avenue and Fayette Street, and the Moores opened a funeral parlor at the First Avenue location. In recent years, the property has been transformed into a beautiful Italian restaurant owned and operated by members of the Viggiano family, although the property is still owned by the Moore family. (Below, photograph by Brian Coll, 2004.)

In 1930, Conshohocken was a thriving steel town with many drinking establishments. According to the 1930 census, the borough had 17 registered hotels, including Harrolds Hotel, located on West Elm Street. Harrolds was one of the more upscale hotels in the borough, with a beautiful interior bar and lobby. A modern office complex now occupies the former site of Harrolds. (Left, photograph by Brian Coll, 2004.)

onshohocken has had five bridges
across the Schuylkill River since
1833. A covered bridge existed from
1833 to 1866 and an iron bridge
from 1869 to 1919. A temporary bridge
was built while a concrete bridge was
under construction from 1919 to 1921.
The concrete bridge opened in 1921
and was demolished in 1985, and the
current bridge opened in 1987. This
photograph from the mid–1980s, just
before demolition, shows traffic waiting
to cross into West Conshohocken.
Notice the old woolen mills to the left
and that there are no office buildings
in sight.

Chapter 4

BRIDGES

In 1741, Peter Matson purchased 179 acres of ground on the West Conshohocken side of the Schuylkill River (*schuylkill* is a Swedish word meaning "hidden river"). Matson built his home at the crossing of Ford and Front Streets in the village that later became West Conshohocken Borough. He created a ford with large rocks and wood planks to cross the Schuylkill River (hence the name Matson's Ford). Nearly 100 years later, a bridge company purchased the ground and built a covered bridge 520 feet long and 25 feet wide at a cost of more than $11,000. The covered bridge (above) started assessing tolls in 1838, charging 1¢ for every foot passenger, 3¢ for every horse or mule, and 6¢ for every score of sheep. In 1886, Montgomery County purchased the Matsonford Bridge Company, and after 48 years of paying tolls to cross the bridge, tolls were no longer required. The covered bridge was torn down in 1867 and was replaced by a steel bridge. The steel bridge lasted more than 50 years. In 1919, it was demolished to make way for the concrete bridge.

In 1919, work began on a concrete bridge that was hailed throughout the state of Pennsylvania as an engineering masterpiece. The concrete bridge was imploded in 1985, making way for today's bridge. The three photographs on these two pages were taken from the West Conshohocken side of the bridge, highlighting the borough of Conshohocken in the background.

In November 1921, the new Matsonford Bridge was dedicated, constructed at a cost of nearly $500,000. In November 1987, the current bridge had a grand opening. The construction ended ahead of schedule, and at nearly $7 million, the bridge came in just under budget. A far cry from the cost of the very first covered bridge built back in 1833 for $11,000. The view coming off the bridge on the Conshohocken side of the river has changed dramatically since 1921; dozens of retail stores have been replaced with office buildings and parking lots. (Left, photograph by Brian Coll, 2004.)

There is always a parade or an event going on in Conshohocken. Shown in 1985, the Conshohocken Catholic Youth Organization (CYO) is busy holding a Christmas party and dance at the Conshohocken Fellowship House.

Chapter 5

PARADES AND EVENTS

The borough of Conshohocken and the borough of West Conshohocken celebrated the Matsonford Bridge openings with parades, speeches, and celebrations in 1921 and again in 1987. On November 11, 1921, the boroughs celebrated the opening of the new bridge with a parade, shown with dignitaries marching toward West Conshohocken. On November 27, 1987, 66 years later, a parade is shown crossing the Matsonford Bridge into Conshohocken. (Above, photograph by La Tour Photo Services, 1921; left, photograph by Brian Coll, 1987.)

In 1950, children lined Fayette Street and sat on the curb to watch one of several centennial parades. More than 45 years later, borough children were sitting on the curb at Eighth Avenue and Fayette Street to watch the VFW State Convention Parade, hosted by Veterans of Foreign Wars Post No. 1074 of Conshohocken.

Parades in Conshohocken have been around for more than 100 years, including this 1918 parade with a marching band as it passes First Avenue on Fayette Street. The small building on the corner was demolished in 1919 to make way for the Riant Theatre. In the 1990s picture to the left, Conshohocken spectators line Fayette Street at East Eighth Avenue to enjoy another parade.

Conshohocken has become known as "the Parade Capital of Pennsylvania," as seen in May 1950. Members of the armed services march in the borough's centennial parade just below Fourth Avenue in front of Dr. James Hargreaves's office at 324 Fayette Street. Fifty years later, in May 2000, members of the Conshohocken fire department march in the borough's sesquicentennial parade.

Conshohocken has never had the largest police department in Montgomery County, but the police officers were always the best dressed. The officers posing in the 1920s are, from left to right, Harry Snear, Walter Phipps, Francis "Bunny" Blake, Patrick Donovan, Frank Stallone, and Zeak Kirkpatrick. In the photograph to the left, Conshohocken officers pose at the newly dedicated police monument in Norristown in May 1995. From left to right are James Carbo, George Metz, Walt Speck, Mike Oirler, James Dougherty, Ed Williamson, Paul Price, Michael Kelly, and Anthony Santoro. The monument is dedicated to all Montgomery County police offices who gave their life in the line of duty, including Conshohocken police officer Eugene "Chick" Lucas, who lost his life on August 13, 1917.

The Fellowship House opened its doors to the community on December 18, 1953, and was built at a cost of $250,000. "The Fell," as it is known, recently completed renovations that cost $3 million. Staff members include, from left to right, Charles Mascio, Paulette Trainer, Darlene Hildebrand, Gloria Scott, Brian McCann, Dan Nolan, Jim Sheedy, Floyd Shaffer, and Frank Zoltowski. Members of the Conshohocken playground staff in this 1920s photograph are, from left to right, Frank Staley, Marian Garrett, and Ray Geist. (Right, photograph by Brian Coll, 2004.)

Conshohocken's Soap Box Derby roots go back to 1938, when Walt Cherry won the borough's very first derby race. In 1957, Tommy Carroll raced for the first time, as shown in this photograph, and he won a championship in 1959. Notice the seven-foot-high starter ramps. Forty years after Carroll won his race, Alicia Marie Moore, shown on the right of the photograph with her brother Adam, won the championship and the right to compete in the national race held in Akron, Ohio. When Carroll won in 1959, females were not permitted to race. The Soap Box Derby slogan was "the Greatest Race in the World for Boys." In a court decision handed down in the early 1970s, females were permitted to race, 40 years after the race's inception. (Above, photograph from the collection of Jack Coll; left, photograph by Jack Coll, 1999.)

For more than 125 years, Conshohocken has been a town that has thrived on sports. Residents have celebrated championships and winning seasons, such as the Men's Athletic Association tug of war team that won four consecutive championships from 1907 to 1910. The Montgomery County champions included John Fitzgerald, manager John "Ace" Reilly, James McDade, Joseph Kelly, and "Big Phil." This photograph was taken outside Conshohocken's very first schoolhouse, located on Forrest Street. In the photograph to the right, members of the Plymouth Whitemarsh Colonials basketball team celebrate a state championship in the mid-1990s. John Salmons, a member of the squad, currently plays for the Philadelphia 76ers. (Right, photograph by Jack Coll.)

Potts Quarry, located in Whitemarsh Township just off Butler Pike, produced blue marble, a marble used to build the base of Philadelphia's city hall and many other historic buildings in and around Philadelphia. Once the quarry filled with water, it was used many times as a backdrop for silent moviemakers, and it was a great recreation spot for local residents. Ice-skating was very popular, as seen in here. (Photograph courtesy of Joseph Leary, 1907.)

Howard Laverty dives from the quarry peak in the photograph below. Today, Sherry Lake Apartments wrap around the quarry. On the right-hand side of the photograph, the famous peaks can still be seen. (Below, photograph courtesy of Harold McCuen, 1916; right, photograph by Brian Coll, 2004.)

Conshohocken's organized youth sports have been around for more than half a century. Little League Baseball was formed in Conshohocken in the spring of 1955, and a football league was started in 1961. James "Pat" Mellon, burgess of Conshohocken, opened up the Little League season in 1958 by throwing out the first ball at the Little League field, then located behind the Conshohocken Bocce Club on West Third Avenue. Members of the league include, from left to right, Franny Carr, Joseph Novak, Emedio Cardamone, Art Andrey, Louis Cappelli, Mellon, and Bob Carroll. The more recent photograph shows the Conshohocken Golden Bears midget football team celebrating after winning the 90-pound championship game, defeating Pen-Del 13-6. The Bears' 90-pounders went undefeated in 1990 and enjoyed a lot of support from the cheerleaders. (Left, photograph by Jack Coll, 1990.)

In 1961, the Conshohocken Fellowship House sponsored ice-skating at Mary Jane Sutcliffe Park, where a number of Conshohocken youngsters can be seen warming up around the campfire. Forty-two years later, children show off their trophies from the Fellowship House sponsored summer basketball league held at the park. Although the borough no longer provides ice-skating for area residents, the Fellowship House still makes good use of the basketball courts along with the rest of the park. (Right, photograph by Jack Coll, 2003.)

In the early-20th-century view above, members of the Conshohocken band, led by Leonard B. Smith, assemble on Fayette Street just below Second Avenue. The band traveled to the train station to lead a visiting football team on a parade up unpaved Fayette Street to the football field located at 11th Avenue and Harry Street. Below are the Trammps, an internationally known Philadelphia-based disco group who turned out such hits as "Turn Back the Night" and "Disco Inferno" (from the movie *Saturday Night Fever*). Some members of the Trammps lived in Conshohocken for a brief time. Mayor Robert Frost caught up with the band and posed with them in an ally behind Jack Coll's former studio at 515 Fayette Street. (Left, photograph by Jack Coll.)

Members of the Washies Sirens Band (below) jam away on the third floor of the Washington Fire Company at the 1929 banquet. Pictured, from left to right, are Alan Carter, Chick McCarter, Mike Nally, Ed Cavanaugh, and Henry Sauter. In the photograph to the right, music fan Bob Caucci (left) and Mayor Robert Frost (right) pose with music legend Billy "the Human Percolator" Harner. Harner appeared at Tillies Bar in Conshohocken and was known for his smash hit "Sally Saying Something."

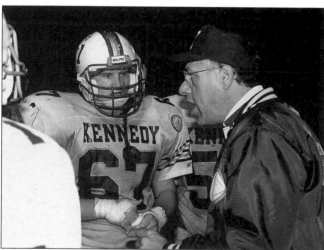

In the mid–1950s, members of the Conshohocken High School football team run out onto the A. A. Garthwaite Field, also known as the A Field, located at 11th Avenue and Harry Street. In the early 1990s, former Archbishop Kennedy School football coach Chris Bockrath takes time out during a game at the A Field. The field was built in 1914 and is still used today. Conshohocken High School closed in 1966, and Archbishop Kennedy closed its doors for good in 1993.

Conshohocken has always been a flag-waving patriotic small town, as seen in this 1950 centennial photograph taken in front of the Washington Fire Company. Members of the fire company and local residents show support by draping flags and banners over the firehouse. Forty-five years later, residents young and old are shown waving flags during a loyalty day celebration in front of Conshohocken Borough Hall.

More than 50 years ago, members of the St. Matthew's High School cheerleading squad posed for this photograph. Pictured, from left to right, are Jean Rath, Kathleen Davidson, Joan Murray, Mary McNeelis, Jane Frease, Julia Nowak, and Rita Janifer. More recently, members of the Conshohocken Golden Bears traveling cheerleading squad pose with members of the Philadelphia Eagles cheerleaders at the 2004 mayor's Special Events Committee annual car show. (Left, photograph by Brian Coll, 2004.)

For many years, Conshohocken held a May Day at the Conshohocken A Field, where all the borough's children would come together for a day of fun, including games, contests, Easter egg hunts, and other forms of recreation. The photograph below, taken on May 15, 1953, shows children in the bleachers waiting to find Easter eggs. In 1993, the borough's children came together for the dedication of the Aubrey R. Collins Park. Members of the St. Paul's Baptist Church youth choir sang "Heart to Change the World" at the dedication. Aubrey R. Collins was a well-liked young man who grew up on Elm Street and passed away too soon. The park was dedicated in his memory and serves as a tribute to all young residents.

Conshohocken residents love parades, as seen in this 1953 photograph in which residents line up near Fourth Avenue and Fayette Street just outside the post office, waiting for the parade to go by. More than 40 years later, residents gather at 11th Avenue and Fayette to enjoy the VFW State Convention Parade. Sitting on the lower step are Michelle Stiteler, one-year-old Lauren Stiteler, and the dog Bear. The others are, from left to right, Kristin, Ann, and Jane Love; Meaghan McCabe; and Scott Stiteler.

In the mid–1980s, the Washington Fire Company hosted one of the many parades they sponsored. Riding in the 1924 pumper fire truck is the grand marshal of the parade and a member for 60 years, John "Chick" McCarter, with Frank Carlin (driving).

Chapter 6

SCHOOLS AND FIRE COMPANIES

The Washington Fire Company has been fighting fires for more than 130 years. Founded in 1873, the fire company has provided a continuous service to the community. The photograph above was taken in 1900 in the basement of the original firehouse, located on West Hector Street. The last names of some of the members are Jones, Stemple, McCarter, Mason, Shaw, Garnett, Dunlap, Bailey, and Stott. The photograph to the left was taken 100 years later, during the Pennsylvania State Fireman's Convention. Included in the photograph are members Frank Carlin, Dave Zinni, Mike McGrath, Joe Januzelli, Joe "Bounce" Wertz, Andrew Carlin, John McGrath, Beth Januzelli, Wayne Birster, Jean McGrath, Tina Reese, Anthony D'Angelo, Bob Zinni, Roseanne Oshinski, Anthony Davis, and Rea Januzelli (the company's oldest member). (Left, photograph by Jack Coll, 2002.)

Conshohocken Fire Company No. 2 proudly displays their apparatus in 1925, which included two ladder trucks and an ambulance, at the corner of Harry Street and East Ninth Avenue. In 2004, the fire company once again displays their apparatus in their new firehouse, now located in the 800 block of Fayette Street. (Right, photograph by Brian Coll, 2004.)

SE HOUSE OF FIRE CO. NO. 2. CONSHOHOCKEN. PA. DEDICATED MAY 12. 190

Conshohocken Fire Company No. 2 was founded in 1903. In the photograph above (taken in May 1906), members of the fire company pose outside their newly built firehouse, located on the corner of East Ninth Avenue and Harry Street. In May 2004, members of the No. 2 fire company proudly pose in front of their newly built firehouse now located in the 800 block of Fayette Street. (Left, photograph by Brian Coll, 2004.)

Conshohocken High School was built in 1913 on the southwest corner of Seventh Avenue and Fayette Street. An addition of 14 classrooms was added in 1925. It is believed that this photograph was taken in the mid-1930s. There were more than 1,200 students in attendance at the school. The high school was closed in 1966, due to a Pennsylvania state mandate that all schools below the required attendance were forced to merge. Conshohocken merged with the Plymouth and Whitemarsh school districts. Conshohocken High School had 379 students when it closed its doors. Montgomery County Community College used the school for five years until a new county facility was opened in Blue Bell. The building was demolished in the mid-1970s.

A bank was built about 10 years later and is currently occupied by Sovereign Bank. (Above, photograph by Brian Coll, 2004.)

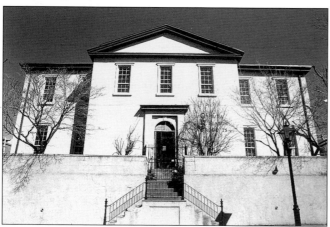

St. Matthew's High School, pictured c. 1913, was located in the 200 block of East Hector Street and was built in 1872 at a cost of $15,000. Over the years, the building served as the elementary and high school for St. Matthew's Church. Although a new school was built on Fayette Street in the 1930s, the Hector Street school was used until the 1960s, before it was sold. The building was used for industry for a number of years and is currently being converted into apartments. (Left, photograph by Brian Coll, 2004.)

More than 60 years ago, students waited to cross the street under the direction of a crossing guard. The public school system was established on May 15, 1850, the very day Conshohocken was incorporated. The Harry Street school was built in 1869 and later named the Hoffecker School in honor of Reuben Hoffecker, Montgomery County's first school superintendent. The Hoffecker School was rebuilt in 1958 with funds provided by Hervey S. Walker and was renamed in his honor. In the mid-1980s, the school was renamed to its current name, Conshohocken Elementary School. Students cross Harry Street under the watchful eye of principal Dr. Patricia Medeira, Michele Gilbert, and Valerie Ward, pictured from left to right, on the final day of school in 2004. (Right, photograph by Brian Coll, 2004.)

The Peoples Drug Store, once located at 301 East Hector Street, was owned and operated by Samuel and Rachel Katz. The Katzes opened the store in 1931 and served the residents of Conshohocken for more than 50 years before closing it in 1975. Samuel Katz is seen on the left in this 1927 photograph holding hands with his son Eugene. Pharmacist Sol Aurbuck is on the right. Eugene went on to become a dentist, along with his brother David. The two shared a medical office with their brother Dr. Robert Katz. They practiced at Fifth Avenue and Fayette Street for more than 50 years. The Hector Street site is now occupied by townhouses.

Conshohocken has been blessed with many great organizations over the years, and perhaps one of the leading service organizations in the past quarter-century has been the Conshohocken American Business Clubs (AMBUCS). Chartered in November 1979, the AMBUCS has helped countless organizations since. Shown below are, from left to right, the following: (front row) Bill Reifsnyder, George Falcanero, Bill Rex, Richard DiCurcio, and Jim Steno; (back row) John Reifsnyder, Lee Zolkowski, Joe DelBuono, Dave Bowe, Tom Bracken, Peter Moore, and Tom Kilinski.

Chapter 7

ORGANIZATIONS AND CHURCHES

Members of the Conshohocken Grand Army of the Republic post are shown outside their headquarters in 1907. Located on the northeast corner of Third Avenue and Forrest Street, the headquarters was built in 1890. The Conshohocken branch of the Women's Christian Temperance Union (WCTU) had the building erected, and for more than 114 years, the building has been home to churches and businesses. The WCTU conducted business in the building for more than 15 years, followed by a military post, a printing shop, basketball leagues, and (in 1980) St. George Coptic Orthodox Church. In recent years, the building was purchased and used as the business offices of Laken, Kramer, Cafiso & Associates. (Above, photograph courtesy of Sam Webster, from the collection of Jack Coll, 1907; left, photograph by Brian Coll, 2004.)

St. Mary's Church, established in 1905, was started with about 100 Polish families who came to Conshohocken to work in the steel mills and worsted industries. Early masses were celebrated at the Wood residence, located at Oak and West Elm Streets, before a former Presbyterian church was bought and renovated at East Elm and Maple Streets. In 1949, members of St. Mary's parish broke ground for their new $250,000 church. More than 500 parishioners attended the ceremony. The former church was demolished to make way for a parking lot. (Below, photograph by Brian Coll, 2004.)

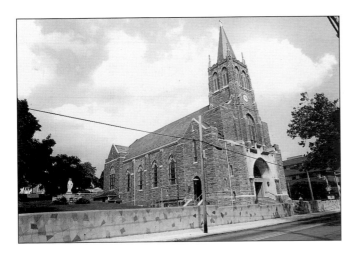

The Calvary Episcopal Church was founded on July 25, 1858. Early church services were held in Stemple's Hall, located on Forrest Street. The original church was built in 1859 on the southeast corner of Fourth Avenue and Fayette Street, and the parsonage, shown on the right, was built in 1873. The original church was demolished in 1888, and ground was broken for the current structure, which was completed in 1889. The parsonage was demolished in the 1960s. (Left, photograph by Brian Coll, 2004.)

St. John's African Methodist Episcopal Church, located in the northeast corner of Eighth Avenue and Harry Street, has been a staple in the borough of Conshohocken since 1880. In the 1973 photograph below, members of the choir pose outside the front doors of the church. Since that time, members of the church have made great strides, building a beautiful addition to the church several years ago while membership in the church has remained strong. (Right, photograph by Jack Coll, 2004.)

In 1851, Catholic bishop Francis P. Kenrick sent Rev. James Maginnis to Conshohocken to establish a new parish. Under Maginnis's leadership, members soon erected a church on the corner of Harry and Hector Streets. Maginnis named the new church St. Matthew's. In 1863, a school was opened in the basement of the church. In 1915, St. Matthew's Church purchased ground owned by James Gibney at Third Avenue and Fayette Street to build the current church, which was dedicated on September 21, 1919. Now, an office building occupies the lot at Harry and Hector Streets. (Left, photograph by Brian Coll, 2004.)

The borough of Conshohocken was 18 years old when the First Baptist Church was formed in 1868. A few years later, the congregation built a beautiful church on the northeast corner of Fourth Avenue and Harry Street. Notice the gas lamp hanging down in the middle of the intersection and the hitching post on each corner in this 1898 photograph. Today, Rev. Bradley E. Lacey is the pastor. (Right, photograph by Brian Coll, 2004.)

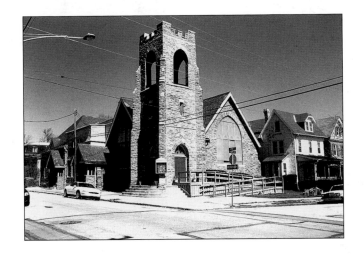

In the early 20th century, traveling churches were very popular. A religious faith group would pull into town and stay for one to six weeks. One popular church that managed to stay a little longer was the Evangelist Church, then located on the southwest corner of Second Avenue and Forrest Street. A private residence occupies the site today. (Left, photograph by Brian Coll, 2004.)

The greatness of Conshohocken can be traced directly to the volunteer organizations that have served and continue to serve the residents. In the 1919 photograph below, members of the Millionaire's Club pose on the Fourth of July outside their headquarters, located in the Meadows along the river, the former site of Hale Pumps Foundry. Members include Harvey Shaw, Fred Lukens, Kid Johnson, Jim McCally, Bill Lukens, and a Mr. Bergey. One of the strongest organizations in the borough, the Conshohocken AMBUCS recently celebrated their 25th anniversary. This photograph of the AMBUCS was taken in the mid-1990s at their annual Thanksgiving Day meeting. (Right, photograph by Jack Coll.)

Shortly after the borough was incorporated in 1850, the need for a street department was evident. Very few streets were planned and developed in the borough before the beginning of the 20th century. The street department around the turn of the century consisted of hired residents who helped level the dirt and stone streets to allow safe passage for horses and wagons and the new motor coach. Today's public works department is pictured, from left to right, as follows: (front row) Ralph J. Gambale, Daniel R. McArthur, Derrick L. Haley, Richard G. Stingle, and Robert J. Ambs; (back row) Robert "Moe" Keys, Robert E. Phillips, Francis Perry Jr., and Mike Maxwell. Public works superintendent Harvey Buek Jr. is sitting in the cab of the truck. Both photographs were taken on Forrest Street, just below Second Avenue. (Left, photograph by Brian Coll, 2004.)

Politicians just love to shake hands. In the late–1970s photograph below, the mayor of Conshohocken, Francis Ruggiero (left), shakes hands with Frank Rizzo, mayor of Philadelphia, while Conshohocken councilman Ed Drabb looks on. In the mid–1990s, Conshohocken councilman Vince Tataro shakes hands with First Lady Hilary Clinton while Conshohocken police chief James Dougherty looks on. (Right, photograph by Jack Coll.)

In 1960, John F. Kennedy made a brief stop in West Conshohocken and spoke to a small crowd. With a light rain falling, Kennedy tried to convince the crowd that he was the right man to serve as president. More than 40 years later, Pres. George W. Bush made a stop in Conshohocken. With a soft rain falling outside, Bush was more than happy to talk, joke around, and sign autographs with members of the O'Neill family. (Left, photograph by Jack Coll, 2002.)